ALSO BY MARK TERRILL

Mark Terrill

THE UNDYING GUEST

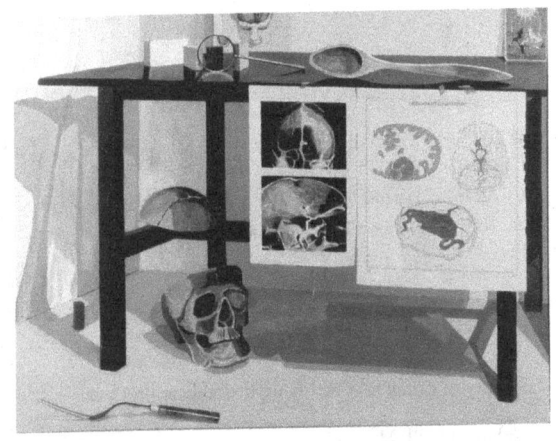

SPUYTEN DUYVIL
New York   Paris

Library of Congress Cataloging-in-Publication Data

Names: Terrill, Mark, author.
Title: The undying guest / Mark Terrill.
Description: New York ; Paris : Spuyten Duyvil, [2023]
Identifiers: LCCN 2022053719 | ISBN 9781959556084 (paperback)
Classification: LCC PS3620.E765 U54 2023 | DDC 811/.6--dc23
LC record available at https://lccn.loc.gov/2022053719

Faith doesn't come from security.
It comes from survival.
    —Ken Kesey

LOOKING UP

Looking up from my plate of fried noodles in a Korean restaurant in Hamburg at the bustling intersection & puddle-dodging pedestrians I notice a Rasta-looking black guy & a yuppie-looking white guy striding across the street shoulder to shoulder oblivious to the rain talking & nodding & emanating a cool forbearance with mellow yet knowing smiles & halfway across the street they're shaking hands on some kind of spontaneous agreement while still striding along & there's something I like about what I'm seeing & the message I think I'm receiving the one about fraternity & brotherhood & bridging cultural gaps & people coming together for the sake of coming together & I'm so caught up in thinking that I almost don't see the tiny packet of dope slipping through their fingers & the wadded-up euro notes slipping back in the other direction all so smooth & graceful & polished & practiced that it's actually a kind of art in itself & *hey* that's good that's fine I *like* art because art always makes you think about what you're looking at whether you actually understand it or not.

The Convergence

A crystalline day in late September standing on the bank of the Kiel Canal in Hochdonn watching the little ferry traversing back & forth then two big freighters approaching from opposite directions passing each other directly underneath the giant railroad bridge superimposed against the grain elevators & the bright blue sky & the huge bluffs of cloud beyond which can be seen a distant jet leaving its lone wispy trail across the firmament in the very same moment in which a train is crossing the bridge with a deafening metallic drone & suddenly I'm aware of myself at the center of this transit-convergence-influx trying just to be open to the onslaught of input trying just to be as present as possible in the unfolding moment converging & merging with the sum of my surroundings until there's no longer any concept of me separate from where I am or the space that I'm occupying just one big gradually expanding confluence which perfectly provides the answer to that hypothetical question *What would all this look like if you didn't know what it was?*

SOMETHING RED

Eighty-two degrees in downtown LA the sky the color of chicken broth with a splash of milk in it walking down Broadway turning into Fifth Street something red catching my eye turning to look through the plate-glass window of the Lisa Beauty Salon seeing a kid just barely old enough to stand up draped in a bright red smock so that only his head is protruding looking a little unsure standing there in his mother's lap in the barber chair while she looks on with a mixture of pride trepidation & motherly concern as the woman with the big electric hair clippers shaves the kid's head with gentle purposeful strokes & the kid is looking up at the woman with the clippers with an expression of complete trust & even *enjoyment* leaning into the strokes of the buzzing clippers like a cat leaning into your hand as you pet it the fine silky black hair falling away in wispy black shards the kid's eyes wide with attentive pleasure & I'm standing there on the sidewalk a frozen figure amid the streaming flux of passing pedestrians totally transfixed by this tableau of benevolent domesticity & its subtle message of the genesis of faith.

The Kiss

Early Monday morning the night train from Hamburg pulls into the Gare du Nord in Paris & I step down from the train & make my way through the crowded bustling station & emerge through the front doors & am confronted with the spectacle of intense rush-hour traffic now almost at a standstill making the place de Roubaix seem like a giant sea of sheet metal or a vast cubist-futurist collage accompanied by honking horns & idling motors & clouds of exhaust & the staccato rattle of jackhammers & the piercing blasts of the traffic policemen's whistles as they attempt to maintain a semblance of movement through the obstacle course of barricades set up by the street department who have torn up huge sections of the street for some expansive construction project while people are loading & unloading luggage from cars & taxis & pedestrians are streaming in & out of the station working their way through the maze-like ever-shifting gridlock while delivery drivers & motorcycle couriers are vainly struggling to inch ahead as the collective tension increases exponentially becoming a palpable pulsing presence & then I catch sight of a young couple standing beacon-like in the middle of the stagnating chaotic scenario locked in an embrace apparently totally oblivious to their surroundings deeply immersed as they are in the sensual pleasures of a prolonged & passionate kiss putting a particularly Parisian-romantic spin on the otherwise harrowing reality of another Monday morning in the grinding-to-a-halt City of Light.

REVERSE ANGLE SPECULATION

It could be cold it could be windy it could be one of those big bright blustery sunny afternoons in San Francisco with jagged chunks of cloud blowing in off the Pacific right over the rooftops of North Beach the day intersected with angular shards of refracted light & bus exhaust & swooping gulls & bay smells & ambulance sirens & countless other sensual stimuli coming in from every possible direction at once although you wouldn't necessarily be aware of it all what with the sky so big & blue & inviting that you're thinking you could just step right through it to some "other side" where things might be entirely different perhaps not necessarily better or worse maybe even just exactly the same as they already are "here" which would of course be sort of weird going all that distance going through all those changes just to find yourself right back where you were in the first place "as though" you'd never been anywhere else at all.

THE RUSH

The rush of ideas while streaking down the autobahn in a glossy black Nissan Primera approaching Hamburg at 150 kilometers per hour each idea & its attendant imagery displacing the next in a rapid-fire scenario of shunting wants & desires & empty speculation about the meaning of the past the significance of the present & the contingency of the future while the *Star Trek*–like TV tower pierces the blue sky above the city skyline & a skein of cottony clouds comes coasting in from the west casting a ragged patchwork of shifting shapes of light & shadow across the green fields & pastures surrounding the city mirroring exactly the random pattern of thoughts concerning mortality & immortality the relevant & the irrelevant the important & the unimportant until it's like one big rotating radar dish of consciousness taking in all the myriad signals at once at a speed much too fast to process rapidly becoming an infinite cerebral blur of cognition a freeze-frame rush of stroboscopic synapses a shuddering loop of perpetual departure & interminable transit.

A Passing Glance in the Open Door

A passing glance in the open door of the bedroom while heading toward the bathroom & seeing the tossed-aside covers on the bed & catching a brief whiff of the stale slept-in breathed-out air & being struck again with how we're always leaving behind some telltale afterimage wherever we go some imprint some trace some mark however faint or tenuous it might be which on the one hand serves to confirm our at-times-questionable existence on the material plane but on the other hand also heightens & intensifies the true temporality of it all by foregrounding & making plastic the very physical dependency of our beings & in turn automatically triggers further future speculative scenarios in which there will be no more tossed-aside covers no more stale slept-in breathed-out air or any other signs whatsoever of our existence which could almost be a sobering yes even *frightening* realization if it wasn't simultaneously outweighed by such an overwhelming sense of utter & final relief.

The Favor

Hitchhiking through England an old guy picks us up in a red Datsun pickup asks us where we're going notices & comments on our American accents & we climb into the back of the truck huddled in our jackets watching the green countryside & slate-roofed houses & black & white cows flashing by & when we finally reach the roundabout just outside of London where he's heading south he stops on the side of the road & we climb down from the bed of the truck & he comes around back with a thermos bottle in his hand asking if we'd like a cup of coffee before we continue on our way & we both nod eagerly at the same time wondering why all the extra hospitality but not wanting to seem suspicious or ungrateful & as we drink from the steaming plastic cups he offers us some cigarettes as well which we also gladly accept & we stand there drinking strong black coffee & smoking Marlboros & wondering what it is with this guy standing there watching us with such obvious satisfaction & pleasure & as we return the empty cups & make a move to go he starts telling us a story about how he'd been a soldier in World War II & how he'd been cut off from his division behind enemy lines somewhere in Belgium & went into

hiding with no radio no food no nothing for days &
was finally discovered by some American soldiers who
gave him hot black coffee from a thermos & American
cigarettes for which he was forever grateful & that he'd
been waiting all these years for a chance to return the
favor.

THE SWEEP

The optic sweep glides along the horizon of the upper pasture slows down & lingers at the huge oak tree below the muddy spring where the cows are standing knee-deep in black muck then moves slowly across the woodpile & slows to a halt in the stand of ash trees suddenly anchored by something deeply emotive emanating from the blue-green shadows of the ash leaves at the same time totally aware of the improbability of trees being able to emote anything at all knowing full well that it's most likely the work of some lurking consciousness spinning its web of perception cognition & association & ultimately something that is being projected from *within* as opposed to being perceived from *without* but nonetheless it truly seems as though the unidentifiable emotional quality is suspended right there in the leaves of the ash trees rustling softly in the sultry August breeze laden with moisture sucked up from the North Sea prior to the cracking & booming of another evening thunderstorm with all its various psychic triggers & emotional attachments sweeping across the lush green landscape.

THE TIME TIME TAKES

I'm sitting in the Café La Madeleine de Proust in the rue Descartes in Paris on a mild sunny October afternoon having just finished a tomato & basil *tarte* & green salad & a glass of red wine now leaning back in my chair lingering over a cup of espresso aimlessly soaking up the atmosphere admiring the glassy blue sky & the sheen of the black slate roofs & the stalwart stone edifices of the buildings & the cobblestone streets polished to a high gloss from all the endless years of use & eventually my eyes come to rest on the receipt in the little silver tray on the green metal table with its patina of age & spots of rust & reading the name & address I find myself in a quirky interstice where the names Proust & Descartes are overlapping & refracting my perspective & perception accordingly & then I'm thinking about thinking & the time time takes & all that goes with it when it goes & what little actually remains as proof that we are what we are merely because we're able to think about it which in terms of substantiality really doesn't seem like very much at all.

EGGBURGERS

Having just come from our afternoon visit with Paul Bowles & Mohammed Mrabet at the Immeuble Itesa we're sitting outside on a couple of stools at the funky metal counter of Eric's Hamburgers tucked in that bleak little side street just off the boulevard Pasteur in bright dusty sun-colored Tangier waiting for our so-called Eggburgers with the unplanned evening looming languorously ahead of us when a grimy kid in tattered filthy jeans & grubby T-shirt comes up with extended hand & fractured smile hoping to elicit a few dirhams from us but we just shake our heads & sip at our Cokes listening to the sizzling meat & watching how the guy in the cool Eric's Hamburgers T-shirt & little white sailor's cap cracks two eggs into two metal rings on the grill to form the perfectly round fried eggs which he then slips on top of the hamburgers with a deft flick of the wrist & the kid is still there begging relentlessly having moved in right at our sides now tugging at my shirt with that persistent kind of hope & anticipation that seems to know no end but suddenly the cook reaches for an egg & as his hand goes up in the air about to pitch the egg the kid is already running away down the street with a cackling laugh & we watch in kif-induced awe how the egg goes cracking splattering down the street in grainy hyperreal Peckinpah-like slow motion just barely missing the kid whose smile is now much bigger & much more telling than before.

THE MIDST

In the midst of washing the dishes at the kitchen sink I turn to look out the window at a subtle change in the autumn light slanting through the trees along the south side of the upper pasture as another storm front moves in off the North Sea & the greens & the yellows & the browns are subsumed by the grays & the silvers & the blues & glancing down at the cat sleeping peacefully on the chair at the kitchen table within the warming reach of the radiator under the window it dawns on me that despite all the obvious differences between a sleeping cat & a dishwashing man we're both operating on planes of incredible similarity at the core of which is a formula defined by *place* plus *being* which has as its sum *existence* & right away I see that the cat & his existence are actually a mirror-like living metaphor for me & my own existence & that together we reflect an even greater existence which is the collective existence of all beings & all existence & that in the process of doing this we're forming a dialectical microcosm of a much greater macrocosm while simultaneously merging into a huge ever-extending nexus which then transcends all individuality whatsoever bringing into question the very concept of microcosm versus

macrocosm & making me think that maybe this is it—
this is all there is—the one big totality the whole damn
thing right here right now in this farmhouse kitchen in
rural Germany & then I have to lean on the edge of the
sink with my soapy hands while I take a deep breath &
shake my head in incredulous disbelief at the thought
of it all while the cat rolls over & yawns & stretches
with all the languid panache of a true professional as I
get ready to tackle that greasy frying pan sitting there
on the stove as much a part of my existence as anything
else out there.

The Stream

A stream of consciousness comes up out of the subway right there on Alvarado Street flows along MacArthur Park amid the guys on the sidewalk selling baseball caps cigarettes bootleg salsa CDs & phony IDs on past the guy with no legs propped up against the lamppost coolly regarding the proceedings with a steadfast countenance crosses the street at Wilshire passing the old guy handing out the garish red & white flyers for Botanica San Martin Caballero passing by the Jesus freaks yelling themselves hoarse at the portals to the park then flows on past the frazzled stray cat meowing for sympathy past the black guy with the jarred-loose appearance who says *Hey—remember me? I was there when you got out...* past the empty Modelo Especial beer cans lying in a shiny pile past the homeless & unemployed & winos sprawled on the grass or down for the count in the spiky shadows of the tall palm trees fingering the milky-blue opacity of the sky through which cuts an LAPD helicopter with its ratcheting chatter of airborne internal combustion & Orwellian angst moving off toward the southwest where ragged puffs of gray cloud are now blowing in off the windy Pacific Ocean in a silent steady stream.

Paris-Macbeth Vortex

The slightest purpose with its featherweight resolve
has me going down the rue Lacépède from the
place de la Contrescarpe toward the Jardin des Plantes
for a leisurely walk in the park & halfway down the hill
I see two grubby red-faced winos in a little corner niche
between two buildings which provides just enough
shelter for the two of them & their meager belongings &
my passing cursory glance becomes a prolonged study
as I walk by looking closely yet discreetly at how they're
living right there on the street amid the empty bottles
& rubbish & dirty blankets grumbling & muttering
& puttering about in their squalid domesticated
oblivious anarchy which catches me up in a vortex
of conflicting emotions repelled as I am at the filth &
neglect but simultaneously sympathetic toward their
plight & finally almost sort of envious at the display of
such resolute stoicism & overall psychic immunity in
the face of such otherwise hopeless odds making me
think of that scene in *Macbeth* where Banquo comes out
of the castle with his son & makes a passing remark
to the men outside about the impending rain only to
be answered by the flash of a blade & the admirable
four-word sentence so succinct & brutal: "Let it come

down" which of course meant the end of Banquo but also implied something of the fatalistic going-with-the-flow-of-things & spiritual resilience which I could stand to cultivate myself if I wasn't always so caught up in the endless play of appearances & the spectacular imagery while walking down the street in Paris just ghosting along through the thick of it all.

ENIGMATA

Sunday at the beach on the other side of the island some little kids are looking at my spider tattoo admiring it chattering in Portuguese daring each other to move in a little closer maybe even touch it & I can tell by looking in their faces that they're thinking it's the coolest thing ever & bad as hell & then I'm looking around at all the other young firm vivacious incredible bodies & the sagging paunchy over-the-hill bodies & the just plain body-bodies feeling myself caught up in the irrevocable drift of time with all of its manifestations exacting or otherwise & realizing with no small consternation that I am forever & finally cut off from that special sacrosanct place from which an ordinary meager twenty-five-dollar slightly faded spider tattoo can be seen to hold something of the boundless mystery that is slowly but surely effacing us all.

ZORBA THE GREEK BLUES

Late afternoon in a Greek restaurant in Hamburg that lethargic intermezzo between lunch & dinner when hardly anything is happening just the odd customer sitting alone over a plate of gyros & a beer perusing the *Morgenpost* while the family that runs the place is sitting around their regular table in the corner by the door to the kitchen the table still cluttered with the remnants of a late lunch laughing & talking loudly in Greek while a dusty tape deck plays a greasy cassette of the theme music from *Zorba the Greek* for the ten-millionth time & one has to wonder how they can still find what it takes to tap their feet & nod their heads in time to the music which after all those years of endless playing can't possibly retain or even mean all that much of anything except for maybe the most threadbare of lifelines to a rocky island in a bright blue sea far beyond the snowcapped Alps & a lousy Mexican actor named Anthony Quinn.

YOKOHAMA TIME-CONTINUUM MEDITATION

I step out of a big air-conditioned shopping mall in Yokohama into the hot bright Japanese sun looking for a taxi to take me back to the ship & over on the left I notice some old men hanging out on cement benches by a fountain in the shade of the palm trees & at first I think they're just waiting for their wives or kids to come out of the mall with bulging shopping bags & attendant expressions of consumer contentment but when I look closer I see that despite their regular-citizen appearance their clothes are dirty & threadbare & their faces are unshaven & scabbed & the few teeth they have are yellow or gray or broken & that they're all sitting on old folded-up newspapers & no one really pays any attention to them anymore they're just sitting there on the sidelines of life quietly killing time while still holding on to some last sense of decorum & protocol & obviously no one is going to be coming out to meet them & they probably don't have any families at all or even a place to live & then I'm thinking about proud samurai warriors with their strict codes & ethics & the rise & fall of empires & cultures & all the intrinsic contrasts & paradoxes submerged in the passing of time & how it keeps folding back on itself to form a sort of Möbius strip of finite eternity forever repeating itself yet continuously transforming us into new & unforeseen evolutions of ourselves so increasingly alien & unimaginable that it's hard to believe that it's still us—or you—or even me—walking around in Yokohama the last day before the ship sails buying deodorant toothpaste beer & other basic amenities before the long run across the Pacific with its day-in-day-out mind-numbing routine of four hours on watch in the engine room eight hours off sleeping to the sound of whirring blowers & distant churning machinery & getting up to eat chicken-fried steak & chili con carne & corned beef hash watching old Bruce Lee videos or reading battered Elmore Leonard or John le Carré paperbacks or maybe working a little overtime to help fatten the payoff but mainly just to help pass the time the very same time that is gradually diminishing each & every one of us.

BECAUSE IT'S FRENCH

The gray wet glistening streets of Paris on a cool November morning through which the complexities of life are moving with their intricate fervor in the form of rumbling traffic & mothers pushing baby carriages & students striding toward the Sorbonne & bent-over old ladies lugging shopping bags from which leeks & baguettes protrude with Parisian matter-of-factness all followed closely by my eyes from behind the big front windows of the Brasserie Le Poliveau where I sit alone at a table as warm & dry & content as a gecko in a terrarium pleased that my broken French & the waiter's somewhat superior broken English allow us a modicum of communication & pleased as well to see how he takes a certain pride in his work which is made all that more apparent as he serves my café au lait & orange juice & omelet with *fromage* & *jambon* with a series of gratuitous yet well-meant flourishes accompanied by snappy little English one-liners like "Yes sir" & "You bet" & later when I'm finished eating & he's clearing the table he asks "It was good?" to which I reply "Excellent" & with a wily grin & a last blast of irrepressible pride he looks at me & says "Because it's *French*" & turns on his heel & leaves me sitting there smiling & looking out the big windows at the endless flow of intricacies no less baffled by it all but definitely much wiser as to the source of certain small contentments.

The Envoy

Dinner over the dishes washed up dried & put away I step out of the kitchen & see a shaft of light from the setting sun shining straight down the hallway gilding the dust motes & illuminating in stark glowing profile the white & black cat quietly eating the last of the dry food in his dish with that stalwart gentle patience & ineffable feline dignity that surpasses anything human I've ever experienced & I find myself caught up in a paralyzing stasis of pure love total devotion & binding attachment while at the same time on a parallel plane of consciousness I'm completely aware of being frozen in this fissure of time this fleeting rapture momentarily cut loose from the ongoing narrative of my existence standing there watching the cat like a giant naked nerve taking it all in registering each & every subtle vibration in the ether of reality while simultaneously realizing the incredible treasure of just *being*.

Compromise Solution

I'm walking down the aisle in a local hardware store looking at the hammers & saws & chisels & axes & screwdrivers barely acknowledging the innocuous ambient background music being piped in through the sound system when the familiar crunching chords & bottom-heavy kick drum & churning beat of the Rolling Stones' "Street Fighting Man" now has my full attention & I find myself singing along surprising myself by knowing all the lyrics by heart at the same time aware of the incredible irony of the Stones' fiery wake-up call being misappropriated by some store manager's strategic thinking as though hearing "Street Fighting Man" is going to put us in the mood to buy some extra sacks of cement or another box of nails the irony of it all quickly expanding transcending morphing into an all-encompassing cynicism as a flashback of memory propels me back to the streets of Oakland California in the late sixties tear gas wafting in the air standing face-to-face with the Oakland police the Alameda County sheriffs & the National Guard forming a barricade between us & the Oakland Induction Center where we're trying in vain to stop the next bus of inductees from arriving prior to being shipped off to Vietnam &

how sure I was that what we were doing was right &
vastly important & the only possible choice in a "free"
society but the inductees were of course inducted &
sent off to their fates & the war was lost & I got older
& "wiser" & wound up in Germany & settled down
& got married & bought a house & now here I am
in this funky hardware store with any & all idealism
having long since been replaced by a sense of quotidian
propriety & consumer complacency & the only real
choice I'm faced with now is between the 4.99 euro
mason's trowel & the 6.99 euro mason's trowel with
the somewhat better-looking handle while Mick blares
out "Think the time is right for a palace revolution, but
where I live the game to play is compromise solution…"
as I quickly decide for the 4.99 trowel & head for the
checkout counter wondering if I can possibly get out of
here with what's left of my integrity still intact.

Sending Off the Godhead
in the City of Light

Time to kill before the reading at the gallery—
walk over to the Seine & descend worn stone
steps in the darkness—fractured shimmer of neon
& streetlamps flickering across the wavelets—over
there two lovers kissing in the shadows—over there
a dope deal going down—over there a lone cigarette
glowing secret agent–like in the inky gloom under the
bridge—& just downstream Notre Dame all ablaze in
the zillion-watt glow of the incessant incandescent full-
fathom perennial millennial non-sustainable fossil-
fuel maximum illumination apparently necessary to
eradicate the brooding darkness in which all our latent
fears might otherwise take root as a party boat motors
by with oblivious revelers unknowingly celebrating the
end of an age not yet named.

THE FLOW

Friday morning wheeling out of the big Ikea parking lot in Hamburg in a post-consumption-backlash state of ultra-heightened awareness hungrily subsuming reality in triplicate & immediately I'm confronted with the distinct yet multifarious aspects of a red-haired girl in an orange jacket on a silver bike turning into a snow-strewn street in which glimpses of shiny anthracite asphalt can be seen through the gray-brown slush where a mailman in a blue & yellow uniform stands on the corner puzzling over some impossible-to-find address in the early-morning madness under a colorless winter sky while the traffic gets heavier & heavier threatening to back up & stall altogether & the stoplight turns green & I slowly ease down the accelerator & merge into what's left of the flow.

A Poem for the Here & Now

Coming up out of the subway into the unusually warm winter sun just across from the gates of the big Jewish cemetery in Prague on a bright Sunday morning I'm the first one in as it opens promptly at nine—the old man in the gatehouse speaks no English but excellent German & gladly answers my query as to the location of Franz Kafka's grave & I go walking down wide paths lined with neatly trimmed hedges & beds of ivy dappled with sun & jagged shadows from the still leafless trees—the constant chirping of birds amplifying the faux-spring-like ambience—all around me the ornate statues & elaborate marble & granite headstones & monuments with names like Goldschmidt Rosenberg & Bernstein & now & then a little official sign pointing the way to *Dr. Franz Kafka* & finally I come around the last corner & there just across from the cemetery wall is the Kafka family plot under a layer of white gravel with a granite obelisk & offerings of candles dried flowers & hastily improvised mementos various trinkets & weathered pages of books with notes scrawled in Japanese Spanish & French & even a little glass wind-chime hanging in the small pine tree next to the headstone adding its soft tinkling to the musical birdsong & the scene is so entirely different than what I'd been expecting—not gritty-gray-neorealistic not film-noir-gloomy not lonesome-foreboding-grim but rather like a pleasant spring day in the park with chirping songbirds & the sun warm on my back under a bright blue sky & looking down to where Kafka is presumably resting in peace under the gravel & earth I suddenly have to wonder just what all that existential angst & inner turmoil was really about—considering how benign & beautiful it all turned out to be—right here in the here & now.

A Poem for Catchers

I leave the house & step into the gray leafless tedium of a winter afternoon in the German hinterlands to take a walk down to the Kiel Canal & right away I feel the fresh air streaming into my lungs & the oxygen permeating my brain & I'm seeing everything with that rare crystalline vision again seeing every tree & fence post & bird & cow & sheep & pheasant & crow & glistening strand of barbed wire in acute minute detail & when I get down to the canal I see that they've been repairing a section of the stone embankment near the ferry slip where the constant wear & tear of the passing ships' wakes has gradually loosened some of the stones & nearby a gray metal construction trailer is parked in which the workers store their tools & eat lunch & crack off-color jokes & along the side of the trailer spray-painted in blue in a crude rolling cursive script are the words *Fuck You* & I stop & stare at the words letting them work their weird magic on me wondering why the hell anyone in Germany would write *Fuck You* in English on the side of a construction trailer by the Kiel Canal & why I was meant to see it & start tripping out about all the inherent *implications* & what it might possibly *mean* but I can't help seeing it as something vastly significant & intrinsically interrelated flashing back to that scene near the end of *The Catcher in the Rye* where Holden Caulfield is at his sister Phoebe's school to drop off a note for her to meet him after school before he hitches out west & how he sees *Fuck You* written on the wall of a stairwell & how it freaks him out because he thinks his sister might see it & ask what it means & have it explained to her all wrong by some pervert & how she might get hung up on it & maybe even end up *worrying* about it & so he rubs it off the wall only to see another *Fuck You* a little while later & yet another *Fuck You* even later until he's going on about how even if you had a million years you couldn't rub out every *Fuck You* in the world & that even when he dies there will probably be a *Fuck You* scrawled below the name on his gravestone & here I am just out for a semi-therapeutic head-clearing afternoon walk suddenly confronted with a mere pair of words which somehow seem so fraught with meaning wondering if Holden Caulfield would feel justified in seeing his two-word nemesis sprayed in blue on the side of a construction trailer by the Kiel Canal more than a half century later or if perhaps I shouldn't get moving before someone comes along & catches me standing here staring at some trivial graffiti in a highly enhanced state of dubious philosophical limbo.

A POEM FOR UNCERTAINTIES

I gave the waitress in the café a fifty & she gave me my
change got sidetracked & left the fifty on the counter
all alone with me & my conscience & I had to dig so
deep down into my frail moral fiber that it hurt & I came
back up emboldened with a spontaneous resolution
to just do good & motioned toward the fifty & the
waitress looked down & shook her head & smiled &
picked up the money & slipped it into her wallet where
it belonged & afterwards out on the street I told you
what happened that I almost earned us an extra fifty
euros which we certainly could have used but instead
got caught up in a tangle of virtue & you said that I'd
done the right thing & that good things would come
my way & I said yeah but you have to *take them* for the
interchange to be complete & we laughed & walked on
down the sidewalk & suddenly I saw the whole world as
a giant garden of crass uncertainties with a knot where
my heart used to be & coffee & beer where the blood
used to flow & the wavering contingencies stacked
up end to end reaching up past the highest tower of
cumulus hovering above the vast city of Hamburg & it
scared me but I got brave & went on.

THE TEN THOUSAND THINGS

Standing by the meat counter in the supermarket waiting patiently in line under the harsh fluorescent lights absent-mindedly looking all the way down to the other end of the building where the dairy products are & seeing that cross-eyed lady who I've come to loathe with the smudgy glasses & blonde frizzy hair stocking the shelves with that obsessive determination of hers & it occurs to me for the very first time just how large & expansive the supermarket actually is realizing as never before the true volume & space involved & all the cans of soup & pet food & rolls of toilet paper & cases of beer & wine & the sheer amount of *things* & suddenly the realization morphs into a sort of allegorical template for all such realizations born from actually observing my exterior environment as opposed to just projecting myself *into* some present situation & generating some kind of internally cogitated abstract-theoretical *presence* thus proving that reality isn't necessarily something you just *think up* but rather something you actually *experience* & that it's not how you fit into reality but rather how reality fits around you that makes you what you are & immediately I think I understand for the first time what Dogen actually meant when he said *That the self advances & confirms the ten thousand things is called delusion; that the ten thousand things advance & confirm the self is called enlightenment* but oh shit look out here comes that cross-eyed lady with the smudgy glasses & blonde frizzy hair giving me a quick dismissive once-over with those shifty eyes while I look away down to my right at the piles of bloody red meat & fleshy-colored sausages glistening in the bleak electric light behind the cold moist glass of the well-attended meat counter.

Laughing Butcher Berlin Blues

From the top deck of a double-decker bus moving slowly through stop & go traffic on the Kurfürstendamm on a cold gray morning in Berlin I glance down into the open front of a McDonald's & see a huge liquid crystal display screen just inside the door where one of those obscene McDonald's promotion-propaganda videos is showing happy cows grazing in luxuriant green pastures & long rows of crispy lettuce under bright blue skies & lush red tomatoes growing in the hothouses & potatoes being harvested & washed & sliced into mountains of french fries & then a shot of a young-looking butcher with longish hair tucked up into one of those disposable paper shower-cap-looking things wearing inexplicably bloodless white clothes & a shiny spotless plastic apron talking directly into the camera while in the background other butchers are handling huge sides of bright red beef in the spic & span ultra-hygienic postmodern interior of some gigantic McDonald's meat processing plant & the butcher kid is going on & on & I can't hear a word he's saying but whatever it is it must be funny because he's smiling & laughing & wow he must be having a great time because he's really cracking up now while the

McDonald's producers are turning up the heat laying it on extra thick trying to put a positive spin on the whole computerized mechanized megadeath cowschwitz reality of what's *really* going on & the last image I see through the shifting barren branches of the trees as the bus slowly grinds ahead is a big close-up of the laughing butcher with his not-so-perfect teeth & fleshy pink lips & a few liquid crystal pimples festering at the corners of his mouth reassuring us that everything's fine yeah sometimes even funny a real laugh riot no blood no fuss no muss no need to burden your conscience with industrial monoculture apocalyptic scenarios or rapacious first-world greed or third-world depravation or exploitation just all those fat fresh juicy lip-smacking super-jumbo technologically wholesome politically correct artery-clogging cardboard-tasting hamburgers by the billions rolling off the end of the conveyor belt faster than a double-decker bus moving down the Kurfürstendamm on a slow gray morning in Berlin.

Approaching Elmshorn

Approaching Elmshorn in the train from Hamburg to Itzehoe on a gray wet windy day with intermittent bursts of blue sky & sunlight I look up from Peter Handke's *Leben ohne Poesie* that I've been reading & see all the trash & litter & colored plastic bags strewn among the silvery leafless birch trees along the railroad embankment some of the plastic bags now just frayed tatters caught in the trees & flapping & snapping in the wind & it isn't so much the sight of all that garbage that is so disturbing—on the contrary—I see it as a colorful kinetic juxtaposition in the otherwise monochrome monotony of the suburban German landscape—but rather that if I were to jump out of the train & go down into the trees & start collecting it would be impossible to gather all of the infinitely innumerable plastic bags & the vacuous absence of closure that thought represents & the cold unsettling bleakness that it brings to me in its momentary realization.

In Terms of Time

In terms of time the city can be celestial the city can be heavenly the city can be nitty-gritty surreptitiously subversive when the city is Hamburg & you're sitting outside the Café Paris in the Rathausstraße on a cool Monday morning because inside it's full & what isn't full is reserved & anyway it's nearly deserted outside & much more in keeping with your all-alone-in-the-big-city state of mind but then a half hour goes dragging by & although you've managed to make eye contact with all three of the young German waitresses who work there—one of them even briefly smiling at you through one of the big open windows with one of those meaningless-empty-gesture-harried-waitress smiles— apparently not one of them has felt compelled to step outside & see what it is you might actually *want* flitting about inside with their Hanseatic reserve & professional haughtiness & part of you is getting all edgy & uptight & impatient in a very small-caliber way thinking *This would never happen in Paris...* while simultaneously another part of you is loosening up & disengaging just taking it all in with a sort of munificent & benign stoicism thinking *Every minute every second the birthing world collides with the dying world & produces the here*

& now... & for that lightning-bolt flash of diamond-cutting wisdom you could almost be grateful if you didn't have such an insuperable hankering for a piping hot café au lait & a flaky fluffy croissant.

A Poem for Those Who Mean Well

There's a big black bug with curved wiggling feelers brown filigree wings & long angular legs crawling across the inside of the kitchen window looking for a way out & not wanting to find myself trapped in a crippling stasis of voyeuristic entropy like John Wieners in his poem "A Poem for Trapped Things" I quickly grab a water glass & a beer coaster & gently & efficiently capture the bug & open the kitchen window & watch him fly out across the pasture toward the canal where some watchful-eyed hungry stork or insatiate bullfrog will probably snap him out of the air before you can say the words *voyeuristic entropy*.

A Poem for Transients

In the Jardin du Luxembourg the Parisians & tourists are soaking up the warm April sun & the chestnut trees are blooming in all their soft glory the trunks now skirted by the dense green foliage of the season's new growth & then there are no more words to describe the scene & I look up from my notebook & watch as an old man ambling by slows down & stops in front of the big fountain amid the whirring blur of activity & billows of dust & splashing & chattering & laughing created by the kids playing with their wooden sailboats in the fountain pool & the way the old man just stands there contrasting old age & evanescence & stasis with the youth & fervor & dynamism of the noisy kids with their sailboats suddenly seems to say everything that needs to be said & without a single loosened word left resonating in the magisterial void.

Up on the Hill

Heading into the post office I first have to step around this older couple in their eighties or older standing outside the entrance & as I look at them in passing I see that he's dressed in an old beret & gold-rimmed glasses & corduroy jacket & jeans with both hands gripping the handles of one of those walkers-on-wheels & I glance over at her & see she's wearing a hat & jacket & white ruffled blouse & a skirt & leaning on a gnarly old wooden cane & together they make a fine picture of elderly dignified sophistication that contrasts sharply with all the farmers & local yokels going in & out of the bakery & the post office & right away I feel a surge of empathy for them & am not even perturbed or bent out of shape because they're standing there clogging up the entrance & just as I'm stepping around them I see the woman looking up at the man with a weird vacant expression & she rolls her eyes & then shuts them & reaches out with a shriveled trembling liver-spotted hand & grasps one of the handles of his walker apparently having a dizzy spell or a moment of weakness & I'm wondering if she's about to faint & whether or not I'm going to have to get involved but then she's just standing there with her eyes shut collecting her composure & gathering her strength & in that very moment as I'm passing behind her I look into the man's face to see how he's reacting & dealing with the situation & in the few intervening milliseconds I simultaneously see the deeply felt concern that a loving trusted partner has for another in such a situation as well as the obvious annoyance that is stirring in him as he thinks *Oh & now she has to go & have one of her spells right here in front of the damned post office* but also visible is the disconcerting naked realization of his own helplessness in the situation unsteady as he is himself with both hands grasping the walker & knowingly unable to catch her if she should fall & the way all those different aspects & emotions & thoughts are being expressed in the eyes & furrows & folds of his lined & weathered face & I'm hit with the realization of how that man could be me & that woman could be you & how just last weekend after seeing *Zabriskie Point* in Hamburg we went to Vasco da Gama for dinner & you were having trouble with your circulation going all white in the face & I was already considering the possibility of leaving although we'd just snagged the best table in the totally full restaurant & no way did I want to leave & how I was feeling all those same exact things that I was now reading in the old man's face & how that was inextricably binding us all together & yet offering no solace whatsoever but rather an ominous taste of all that is yet to come so that finally I have to tear away my gaze from the old man's face but not without a quick final glance at the woman who is opening her eyes & licking her dried lips with her tongue before steadying herself on her cane & taking the first step forward that would lead the two of them down the sidewalk down the hill & into the rest of the day with their faltering but true & tested inexorable determination.

A POEM FOR PARKING LOTS

We're pulling into the mostly empty parking lot in back of the pet store in Itzehoe on a gray north German Wednesday afternoon & over in the corner of the lot is a young man sitting on a curb with a rucksack at his feet drinking a bottle of beer—maybe some homeless guy—or a Polish laborer killing time between odd jobs—but right now just part of the setting & I nose the car into a parking place & out of nowhere you start saying how actually it's a good thing that we all get old & die & that life eventually comes to an end because as you get older & are faced with the ongoing prospect of your own slow decay & the falling away of friends & loved ones it becomes ever more apparent just what's actually in store for you & the thought of dying is no longer fraught with fear & grief but something more like a liberation & even something you could gradually start to look forward to & as we get out of the car I'm thinking hey wow this is pretty heavy & profound for a quick stop in Itzehoe to pick up a couple of spare reflective collars for the cats but then yeah why not & if not now when? & wasn't I thinking the very same thing just the other day? & I say yeah everyone needs something to look forward to & as I'm locking the car & turning toward the back entrance of the pet store I hear you saying that's a nice little piece of property there & I turn to where you're looking & see this empty lot wedged between the back lots & gardens of the surrounding buildings & houses & the whole lot is totally overgrown with nettles & blackberries & weeds & ivy which is crawling up the trunks of the trees all totally neglected & forlorn & yet it's also a perfect picture of nature just left on its own & somehow reassuring in its own weird way & not without a certain morbid charm & I begin to see how it ties in exactly with what you were just saying— although maybe not even intentionally—& even the guy sitting there waiting on the curb with his Zen-like aplomb seems to be a part of the entire metaphysically charged scenario that I've been thrust into with all these signs & signifiers of time & age & what becomes of us all in the interim & I say yeah it is & we turn & head toward the door of the pet store because it's autumn now & the days are getting shorter & the cats are running around out there crossing the street in the darkness & besides all this other stuff we've still got their safety to think about too.

MERGING IN THE RUE BONAPARTE

A tail-end-of-winter afternoon in a café across from Saint-Sulpice an elegant old lady looking a little bored & listless—perhaps a widow in retirement with nowhere else to go & nothing else to do—is horsing around with the hired help—haranguing the waiters—nagging the bartender—berating the owner—all in a playful jocular sort of way—not really getting on anyone's nerves but rather providing a bit of welcome entertainment—now making a big show of preparing to leave—adjusting the scarf around her neck—smoothing her plaid skirt—adjusting her stylishly cut white hair—fussing with her handbag & gloves for the umpteenth time—but still not actually leaving & perpetually postponing her departure the whole thing obviously a regular Sunday afternoon ritual prior to returning to her flat alone to heat up a can of soup & feed some gourmet leftovers to her cat & when she's finally left after a round of farewells & handshaking I'm watching how the bartender & the owner are standing behind the bar apparently talking about the old lady not in a disparaging or pitiful way but in a friendly & respectful manner which in turn bestows me with a warm sense of well-being which I find I'm able to take with me as I pay my bill & step out the door into the chilly early-evening Parisian air & when I glance up at the massive floodlit steeple of Saint-Sulpice profiled against the deep azure of the dusk-tinged sky it's as though the feeling of well-being is suddenly merging with something larger than the church or even the sky itself encompassing everything in a sort of giant embrace which winds me up even further so that I'm flipping up my collar & striding up the rue Bonaparte now so much a part of everything around me that it's actually getting a little frightening & spooky as though my self were on the verge of dissolving entirely & completely coalescing with my surroundings until there was nothing left of me whatsoever—which might not be such a bad thing after all.

Not About Now but Right After

Looking around for the cat I glance out the back window & see instead my black & white high-top basketball sneakers sitting there on the terrace directly in front of the chair where I just took them off maybe five minutes ago before coming inside to bring in the mail which included a copy of Joanne Kyger's hefty collected poems *About Now* & then standing there in the kitchen leafing through that big tome encompassing more than forty years of a life of poetry aware of my head being affected even by the random scanning of various lines so that a few minutes later when I glance out the window & see my empty shoes in front of the chair on the terrace it's as though the person that was me had suddenly vanished from the face of the earth leaving only a pair of paint-spattered high-tops as a reminder of my presence—a Magritte-like neo-surrealist still life which now appears to me like some kind of graphic concrete poem with its deftly embedded message of the sheer evanescence & finite temporality of existence which under any other circumstances might have been a sternly sobering & disconcerting early-morning existential flash but not after looking at all those fine wonderful poems about the vagaries of presence & all its transitory glory & just then the cat comes strolling around the corner of the house stops & looks up at me through the living room window with his cock-eared curiosity & suddenly we're all there again.

SAN FRANCISCO'S FINEST

We get off work at Bethlehem Shipyards & stop by Bouncer's for a beer & down at the other end of the bar these two big hulking fitters are having a loud nasty argument that keeps getting louder & suddenly one of the guys smashes his beer bottle on the edge of the bar & lightning-quick jams the jagged broken bottle right into the other guy's chest & the blood comes squirting out all over the bar & the floor like a bright red pulsing fountain & the woman who tends bar there with the unflappable countenance who's usually so cool is not so cool anymore & even the hardcore welders & riggers are a bit slack-jawed & taken aback & then the cops come screeching up to the curb & the paramedics come howling down the street & the whole place is filled up with serious faces & dramatic demeanors & everyone is exuding that overly righteous barroom concern & totally transparent virtue acting like it was something really evil & terrible but anyone could see just as plain as the peanut shells on the wooden floor that they were actually loving each & every minute of the whole senseless bloody thing relishing at some subconscious level the opportunity to finally be a part of something so seemingly significant in such an otherwise inconsequential existence.

The Afterlives

So you live long enough to become a memory in the minds of those who know you & when you die that living memory is your first afterlife & when all those who knew you die you then enter the next afterlife in which no one ever actually knew you but may have heard about you or read about you secondhand from those who did but are now also dead & when finally all those people are dead & no one is alive who knew you personally or even virtually & nothing remains of you as a memory living or otherwise you then enter the final & ultimate afterlife which is very much like the life that you lived before you lived the life that you're living right now as you read this which is really just one of an infinite number each one following the other forever for a while & sometimes for a very long time.

EVERYTHING HAS TO GO

Strolling along through the flea market in Hamburg where a dark-eyed hook-nosed hag picks me out of the crowd locks us into interminable eye contact holds aloft a battered black answering machine & says in German with a mysterious east European accent *Everything has to go* which to me sounds like a well-worn truism of undeniable collective wisdom hardly worth repeating but what to do with a used answering machine probably still full of other peoples' old messages—*contaminated* like one of those fearsome mythical dirty toilet seats your parents used to warn you about when you were a kid while at another table just a few steps beyond an old empty birdcage with its door hanging ajar suddenly appears as a superbly rendered readymade conceptual installation as though conceived by Sartre & manifested by Duchamp now flashing across the screen of my speculative perception slapping me back into existential sobriety with its sleek metaphorical transmission of the capricious nature of deliverance.

IN THE ALBERT CUYPSTRAAT

Gracefully auditioning for my attention in the street
in Amsterdam at the Albert Cuyp outdoor market
the big gray herons so contrapuntally out of context
stalking boldly on stick-like yellow legs there between
the fish stalls soggy cardboard boxes & garbage in
anticipation of a fallen fish head or a string of bloody
intestines before swooping up over the rooftops &
returning to their hungry broods—their breast feathers
a hoary garland ruffled in the early-morning breeze dark
shiny eyes looking out from beyond the last primordial
wisdom with airs of stoic avian nobility—& like a
rusty boxcar I am shunted through various stations of
psychic transmigration in awe of the herons' bravado
& their cool calculated temerity & Darwinian ability
to adapt while at the same time fearing for their fate
hanging naked in the balance for all to see like Van
Gogh's ear outside the bordello just before a drunken
Gauguin lopped it off with a clumsy swoosh of his
fencing sword & sailed off to Tahiti leaving Van Gogh
to make up the story about the razor & self-mutilation
while Rachel the prostitute took the bloody ear she had
been lovingly bestowed with & tossed it in the garbage
with an impetuous flick of her fine-boned wrist.

A POEM FOR CONTINGENCIES

Looking out the kitchen window I see a black cat crouching aloofly next to a gray & green wheelbarrow & am relieved to see that unlike W. C. Williams's famous red wheelbarrow poem nothing is depending on them for anything at all although a very subtle kind of interdependence is being made undeniably obvious albeit totally independent of any metaphysical projections on my part & thus diametrically opposed to the artificial dependency created by Williams projecting the contingency of the little girl stricken with a fever suspended between life & death whom he is attending to on a house call in New Jersey onto the red wheelbarrow glazed with rainwater by the white chickens in the garden that he can see through a glass door in the girl's bedroom where he sits at her bedside waiting & hoping for the fever to pass & I have to think about how often that poem is misunderstood & misinterpreted as being some sort of cool calculated postmodern tableau—an objectivist riff off of a very imagist setting—when actually it's an extremely subjective poem almost to the point of being selfish since the good doctor is infusing reality with his own personal concerns & thus missing out on the deeper message about the greater interdependence that underlies everything in which each individual implies the whole in its existence while the whole implies each individual in its existence which in turn eventually blurs all borders between the self & the other reducing even the greatest contingency to the subtle sort of interdependence that I'm sure I'm witnessing while looking out the kitchen window at a black cat crouching aloofly next to a gray & green wheelbarrow as my mind tries to convince itself of its immaculate incorruptibility.

PASTELARIA PORTUGALIA

I step up from the black & white mosaic sidewalk along the rua do Galo & into the Pastelaria Portugalia where one drinks little beers & tiny coffees & discusses events quotidian or otherwise with various old cronies or even the cripple at his regular table in the corner where he spoons soup noisily through missing front teeth where one fills out lottery tickets with an avid concentration that approaches the religious or just stops by to buy a loaf of bread a pack of cigarettes & a tin of sardines or stands at the bar sipping beer after beer staring up absent-mindedly at the television where the latest raciest Brazilian soap opera is trundling across the brightly pulsing screen where one notices that the marble-topped tables & old wooden chairs have all been replaced with ugly things of metal & plastic but that's probably the only thing that's changed in the last fifty years or so where the traffic cop with the drooping moustache stands at the bar simultaneously smoking a cigarette & eating a pastry with flecks of white powdered sugar clinging to his black moustache where the bald-headed owner with the dark-ringed heavy-lidded eyes chews on a pencil stub & carefully tallies up the sheet with the credits & IOUs where his overweight son with the easy smile pours brandy with a flashy swirl & always has a dozen saucers & spoons & packets of sugar lined up in two neat rows along the bar where evening glides down unnoticed outside & the cripple has had too much to drink & is annoying the regular customers & finally has to be escorted out the door by the overweight son who shows that he's more than just an easy smile where one gets lost watching the smoke of countless cigarettes wafting upward toward the fly-specked ceiling where it undulates & dissipates & finally drifts away into the encroaching evening & during the time it takes me to walk over to the bar the owner's son has already seen me & is banging the still-steaming espresso grounds out of the steel holder into the worn wooden drawer under the espresso machine & the owner is pulling down the bottle of brandy from its shelf & by the time I reach the bar there is an espresso & a brandy sitting there in front of me without a single word having been exchanged just like all those other days & evenings in the Pastelaria Portugalia there on the corner across from city hall in the rua do Galo.

IMMACULATE PERCEPTION

*B*est whorehouse in all of Panama maybe in the whole *damn world* the taxi driver is assuring us as he mops the sweat from his neck with one hand & with the other steers the clunking rumbling old Chevy Impala with the shot shocks & squeaking springs through narrow streets pocked with potholes & awash with mud & debris after another outburst of torrential summer rains where kids & dogs are sifting through piles of soggy garbage that have collected in the gutters in front of faded pastel-colored buildings with hand-lettered signs with names like Immaculate Conception Pharmacy & in the cab with me are Watkins & J.J. who have taken it upon themselves to introduce me to one of the more fundamental aspects of being a merchant seaman & I've agreed to tag along for a look & maybe for a few drinks but I've also made it clear that I would never be interested in actually paying for sex not that it would be in conflict with my particular moral stance but that it was really just a matter of my preferring the ritual of wining & dining & having the feeling of having achieved something on my own & not just with my money & then we're pulling into the huge parking lot of the Blue Goose—the same Blue

Goose where William Burroughs stopped on his way to South America to search for yagé—which looks like a big blue airplane hangar & we pay the driver & step inside & it's bigger than an Oktoberfest tent & all decked out with bamboo walls & a thatched palm roof & fishing nets suspended from the rafters full of conch shells & dried starfish & glass fishing floats & sitting along the bar are several women of uncommon mind-boggling beauty & Watkins & J.J. & I sit down at a table & are soon joined by three women one of which is without a doubt one of the most beautiful I've ever seen & drinks are bought & jokes are cracked & the afternoon slides comfortably into a boozy evening & though I'm determined to stay faithful to my particular resolution I can feel something tugging at me gnawing at me coming in from some unprotected flank & when Gloria invites me back to her room under the pretense of showing me some pictures in her photo album I'm of course all too aware of the inherent danger but agree to go anyway curious to see what one of these rooms is actually like & much to my surprise it's nowhere as grim as I had been expecting & actually sort of cozy & kitschy & not exactly uninviting & Gloria's is full of stuffed animals & colored lights & shag rugs & pillows & a lava lamp next to the king-size water bed &

whatever it was that was gnawing at me is now eating a hole in me & when I turn to say something to Gloria I see she's already started to undress & now it's more like an acid that is hissing & bubbling & dissolving the last few remnants of my well-intended resolution & as I begin to undress I'm thinking about a lot of things like J.J.'s sagely words of wisdom *You pay for it one way or another* & how getting naked & the jettisoning of conceptual baggage can be intrinsically intertwined & that maybe that taxi driver was actually right maybe this is the best whorehouse in all of Panama maybe in the whole damn world.

ENDURING FREEDOM

From the radio in the kitchen on top of the fridge comes "The Flight of the Bumblebee" as we sit around the silent TV in the living room in winter warming our clammy hands against the burning images of grief, misery, and bloodshed resulting from the wars intended to protect us from all the grief, misery, and bloodshed.

Spleen Machine

There by the tank farm along the Kiel Canal the cashed-in chips of temptation reconfigured through a rain-streaked windshield framing rusty tankers lined up at the fueling docks, a unilateral narrative in which the things themselves are doing all the talking, the flipside of that narrative being the perpetual condition of possibility in which I am invariably the weakest of all eligible participants—swooning, ducking, never even touching the ground—the rabbit-punch-mule-kick of a strange but beautiful young woman's unexpected smile and smooth *Hello* in the fitness studio derailing the quotidian continuity—the disdainful sneer of a skinhead aimed my way while I'm walking up the hill to town—spawning bullet-riddled blood-spurting Charles Bronson Clint Eastwood slow-motion Sam Peckinpah fantasies of vengeance and retribution while the ghost of Gandhi is whispering in my ear to take it easy, not to get all pushed out of shape just because some punk's not liking the way my mojo is working— no reason to get pulled under in yet another riptide of enticement—and in the gray months that precede spring—there in the bathroom mirror each morning— is that a real existent or an actualized possibility?

CHANGE REMAINS SUSPENDED

The emptiness & my placement there—a satiny pocket of transcendental refuge—like leaving the Brasserie Terminus Nord exquisitely satiated with a bellyful of bouillabaisse crossing the rue de Dunkerque in a light evening rain stepping into the bustling Gare du Nord about to catch the next night train out of town ensconced in a womb of pre-departure freewheeling-disconnectedness afloat on a wave of metropolitan ennoblement content with my position in the greater flux of things—the emptiness & my placement there—a satiny pocket of transcendental refuge.

DAYS OF JUDGMENT

The dust on the TV screen is virtually invisible, backlit by the images of blood and shrapnel and the sticky little pieces of someone's brain lying there by the curb where the suicide bomber suddenly bent down to tie his shoe just prior to pressing the switch that would send him to the promised land, the pixels all arrayed in their undying choreography of suspended disbelief.

The Undying Guest

You die again & you're born again & this time around you're the Undying Guest in a room with a hot plate upstairs in back in the Palace of Birth & Death from where you look down at the expansive gardens & neatly trimmed lawns & see the gardener standing by the idling lawn mower trying to decide whether to mow the lawn in parallel swaths or concentric circles as though it was the only game in town & as much as you are able to enjoy being exempt from the contingencies of Time which for the Undying Guest is neither linear nor analog neither finite nor infinite it is not without a certain pang of nostalgia that you watch the gardener standing there caught up in his cloud of ambiguity & indecision like the cloud of nauseating exhaust fumes spewing from the sputtering lawn mower as you remember how it used to be when life was an unbound narrative & closure was its editor & carbon monoxide was something you had to be afraid of & not just a pretty shade of blue hovering there above the deep emerald green of the soon-to-be-mown lawn.

SALVADOR'S LAMENT

Forty-eight hours out of Yokosuka, foaming wake behind us, undulating Pacific Ocean in all directions, wide shimmering blue sky above, last few pesky gulls looking for a handout, deep rumble of giant diesel engines, perpetual turning and churning of brass mass propeller, easy roll of rusty hull, when Salvador, galley personality and dishwasher supreme, looks over at me during our leaning on the railing having a smoke after dinner routine and says, "That new chief engineer has *pierced nipples*, man!" as though this startling unsettling revelation might somehow weigh heavily on our seafaring souls and perhaps even ultimately determine our salty fates, and as much as I'd like to share Salvador's concern, I can only laugh and shake my head and look out toward the precise and glinting seam of the distant horizon and project myself into the not-so-distant future when we'll be docking in San Diego and breaking foreign articles and my six months will be up and I'll be heading down that rattling clanking aluminum gangway with my sea bag over my shoulder and a wallet full of hard-earned paychecks and my mind at ease if not forever then at least for a good long time.

TRANSMONTANE

You can have your restlessness and you can have your mutable modalities deep into the autumn when the spiky green pods of the chestnut trees burst to reveal their glossy brown fruit while riot police crack the heads of saffron-robed monks and mow down protesters in the streets of Rangoon by way of the radio in the kitchen where I stand benumbed in media-minion-paralysis staring out the window at the verdant flatlands stretching toward the North Sea wishing it were the words that were in revolt and not just so revolting.

Memo from Siddhartha

If you can navigate the subway station in Hamburg-Altona climb the stairs and walk through the train station among the infinite flux of faces and figures in that arbitrary barrage of citizens rushing through the early-morning hustle and bustle and come out on the other side still feeling good about it all—with your compassion for humanity still intact—then you don't even need to read *The Flower Ornament Scripture* and can walk on into the park and sit on a bench like Antoine Roquentin in Sartre's *Nausea* staring at the gnarly roots of a chestnut tree where they disappear into the earth and for each and every lack of meaning there will suddenly be a new word in a new language in which you are completely and totally fluent and something like gratitude will well up in your throat as sweet as the nectar going down the gullet of that red-and-green shimmering hummingbird hovering in mid-air over there by those bright pink flowers finely dusted with carbon particles from the diesel exhaust of the trains and buses and other rumbling traffic just on the other side of the ivy-covered wall which separates you from not a single other thing.

THE REFIT

We're docked in a shipyard in Oakland for a major
refit stripped down to a skeleton crew working
a regular Monday-to-Friday day shift & so I'm living
at home on Church Street in San Francisco taking the
bus across the bay each morning doing my gig as deck-
engineer-machinist during the day cashing in on the
extra Subsistence & Quarters pay & hanging out with
my friends at night in the bars of North Beach or south
of Market basically enjoying the setup & there's this
one big black guy named Oliver working as a wiper
on board who often gets delegated to assist me with
a welding job or a repair job in the engine room & I
see how he comes to work each morning decked out in
these exquisite expensive Armani or Brooks Brothers
suits looking sharp as hell & he's got a bit of an attitude
to go along with his look & tends to cultivate a certain
uppity smugness that gets in the way of any attempt
to get friendly with him & each morning he changes
from his fancy suit into his dirty grimy work clothes &
then changes back into his suit when we get ready to
catch the bus back to the Transbay Terminal at Mission
& First & one day after work we get on the bus—
Oliver in a stylish brown three-piece suit looking like

he just stepped out of some posh lawyer's office & me in my greasy dirty jeans sweatshirt grubby jean jacket engineer boots & baseball cap—& we're sitting in the back of the bus going across the Bay Bridge & Oliver takes out his wallet opens it up & shows it to me & there in the little clear plastic window where you would normally see a driver's license is a big pinch of bright green marijuana pressed flat behind the clear plastic & Oliver gives me a look of speculative conspiracy & I nod my head & smile & he rolls up this skinny little joint & we open the windows & smoke the joint ignoring the nasty looks of the bus driver in the mirror & lo & behold it is some of the strongest dope I've ever smoked which hits me full force in what seems like seconds so that right away I have that weird feeling of time simultaneously speeding up & slowing down like trying to run through a giant block of clear Jell-O or aspic & when I look out the windows of the bus I see the ships out on the bay through the vertical cables of the bridge & everything is looking extra grainy & surreal & flattened in perspective as though looking through a big telephoto lens & I realize that I am totally stoned out of my mind & after a jolting series of discontinuous jump-cuts I find myself stepping down from the bus in the Transbay Terminal saying goodbye to Oliver who just nods & smiles & strides off through the crowds at the terminal looking like he's on his way to a rendezvous at the Top of the Mark while I start walking up Mission Street suddenly hyper-self-conscious & acutely aware of my shabby dirty appearance realizing that to anyone else walking down the street I probably just look like any other Mission Street wino grubbing along the street trying to line up another bottle the only saving grace being that no one would ever know or even guess how thoroughly & effectively I'd just been put in my place by some cool cat in a flashy three-piece with an attitude who earns maybe half of what I do.

The Turnaround

I'm walking down the pedestrian-congested Bahrenfelder Straße in Hamburg just passing the Fabrik where I've seen John Cale, Lee "Scratch" Perry, the Mekons & so many other concerts over the last thirty years & then on past the big organic food supermarket swarming with all those super-hip politically correct couples paying horrendous prices for a bunch of grapes flown in from South Africa by a jet spewing its noxious exhaust all across the skies & just as I'm abreast of that big brick office complex housing all the medical practices a ground-floor door swings open & I see this young couple coming out—maybe in their early twenties if even that—looking smart & hip & handsome & well-to-do but not particularly snobby or uptight & maybe even somewhat sympathetic—& suddenly I notice that the girl's face is twisted into this contorted expression of sorrow & grief with tears running down her cheeks & the guy has his arm around her in this very possessive yet comforting way while biting his lower lip in a measured grimace of sheer determination obviously confronted with a whole new kind of challenge & in the very moment that they pass me by going in the other direction I turn & glance

at the sign on the brick wall next to the door & see
that they've just left the office of some gynecologist &
immediately I'm speculating as to the source of all that
grief & sorrow realizing that whatever it is it must be
pretty serious maybe even major & while still walking I
glance back & see the couple stopping on the sidewalk
impervious to the throngs of passing pedestrians & the
guy throwing both his arms around the girl in this big
heartfelt real-deal embrace meant to palliate & assuage
whatever can be palliated & assuaged by such a gesture
in such a moment & I can see by the girl's body language
& overall composure that the well-meant intention of
his gesture is coming through loud & clear & I can feel
my own lagging faith in mankind getting this sudden
boost like a big shot of vitamin B complex for the soul
& I can feel the iron grip of cynicism in which my
psyche usually finds itself ensnared starting to loosen
up & I *know* that those two kids are going to make it
& pull through & get beyond it all whatever it may be
& who knows maybe we're *all* going to make it & pull
through & get beyond it all but certainly not without
the help of someone else who really & truly gives a shit
someone determined not to get turned around by the
vicissitudes & exigencies of human existence someone
prepared to take the extra effort to try to turn those

very vicissitudes & exigencies around & send them
back to wherever they might have come from even if it's
only one single fleeting gesture among all the countless
others on the teeming Bahrenfelder Straße in Hamburg.

ACKNOWLEDGMENTS

Grateful acknowledgments are due to the editors of the following journals, broadsides, chapbooks, and books in which many of these pieces, or versions thereof, previously appeared: *Atlanta Review, Blue Moon Literary & Art Review, BODY, Bombay Gin, The Brooklyn Rail, Buckle &, Center: A Journal of the Literary Arts, Confrontation, Controlled Burn, Diagram, Diner, Facets, Fire, Fractured West, Free Verse, Full Circle Journal, Fulva Flava, Gargoyle, Ginosko, Glowlab, Grasp, Great Balls of Doubt* (Verse Chorus Press, 2020), *Hanging Loose, Heavy Bear, Instant City, Interbang, Jellyroll Magazine, Laughing Butcher Berlin Blues* (Poetry Salzburg, 2010), *Louis Liard Magazine, Mimesis, Mineshaft, Mudfish, The Newport Review, Oranges & Sardines, Orbis, Other Rooms, Paragraph, Pinstripe Fedora, Poetry Motel, Poetry Salzburg Review, The Prague Revue, Prism Review, The Prose Poem Project, The Rambler, Rattle, Red Wheelbarrow, Remark, Rhode Island Roads Magazine, The Salvador-Dalai-Lama Express* (Main Street Rag, 2009), *San Pedro River Review, Sentence, Shampoo, Shearsman, Silk Road, Something Red* (Plan B Press, 2007), *Stride, The Styles, Subtropics, Turntable + Blue Light, Upstairs at Duroc, U.S. 1 Worksheets, Versal, Vlak, Water~Stone Review, Wood Coin,* and *Zen Monster.* "Laughing Butcher Berlin Blues" was excerpted in *Tales of Berlin in American Literature up to the 21st Century,* by Joshua Parker (Brill, 2016). "A Poem for the Here & Now" appeared in *From a Terrace in Prague: A Prague Poetry Anthology,* edited by Stephen Delbos (Litteraria Pragensia Books, 2011). "The Turnaround" appeared in *The Best Small Fictions 2020* (Sonder Press).

MARK TERRILL was born in Berkeley, California, shipped out as a merchant seaman, was a participant in the School of Visual Arts Writing Workshop conducted by Paul Bowles in Tangier, Morocco, and has been a resident alien in Germany since 1984. His writings and translations have appeared in more than 1,000 journals and anthologies, most recently in *The Best Small Fictions 2020* (Sonder Press). Recent publications include a full-length collection of poems and prose poems, *Great Balls of Doubt*, illustrated by Jon Langford (Verse Chorus Press, 2020), a chapbook of poems, *Reframing Oblivion*, with photographs by James LaFratta (New Feral Press, 2021), and a collaborative novel written with Francis Poole entitled *Ultrazone: A Tangier Ghost Story* (The Visible Spectrum, 2022).